GOLF 'N
VERSE

Humorous Poetry & Thoughts on Man's Favorite Sport

By

Dee Burns

PREFACE

I'm Dee Burns and I write verse,
    And some, believe it or not,
I compose while on the golf course,
    And some while on the ... commode.

In Appreciation

To Sara for her persuasion,
dedication, and enthusiasm;
To my friends in Indiana
and Alta Sierra for their support;
To Loraine for her encouragement;
And to Ralph Lee for his advice
and friendship.

Dedication

This book is dedicated to
Jeff and Sandy Chleboun
for helping to make a dream come true. . .
great Pros, great friends,
and great golf!

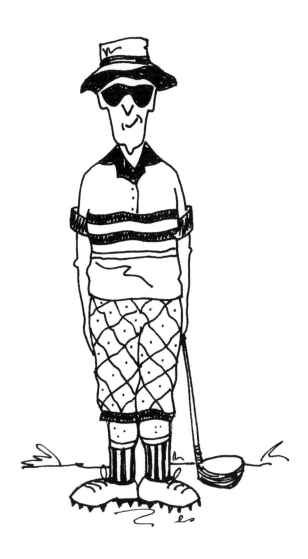

The other day I overheard a couple of ladies talking.

Said one to the other, "Golf isn't a game . . .

It's men in funny pants - walking."

ON THE TEE

LITTLE GOLF BALL

Little golf ball, perched on the tee,
    What's the bond between you and me?

You build me up and let me down,
    Some days I look just like a clown.

You build my ego to the top,
    And other times you let me drop.

You sit there with this fatal lure,
    I'm like an eager entrepreneur.

Most days for you I'd walk a mile,
    If I should miss, you'd wear a smile.

You'd drive a normal man to drink,
    Should we be close, I'd need a shrink.

AFTERTHOUGHTS

When you play golf you become much wiser,
    It's man's great challenge and equalizer.

It rewards you when you're shooting well,
    But miss a few and it's pure hell.

You'd better develop a putting stroke,
    Or prepare yourself to go home broke.

FAVORITE SPORT

Golfing is the only sport
    Where even is called par.
And if your score is less than that,
    They label you a star.

Non-golfers find it most confusing,
    To win with a lower score.
Pros hate the higher numbers,
    No win nor gallery roar.

SCRAMBLING

He hit a ball into the air,
      It fell to earth away out there.

His fairway shot was down the groove,
      With a little draw from follow-through.

But his approach was across a ditch,
      With a trap in front - it was a bitch.

He chose his wedge and hit down through,
      But picked it clean and it really flew.

When it backed up on the rolling green,
      A prettier sight you've never seen.

Then when that putt snaked in the can,
      'Twas a sight to thrill any golfing fan.

LOCAL PRO

Have you ever had the kind of day,
    To give all of your clubs away?

A day when putts won't take the break,
    But your partner runs in a super snake?

The greens won't hold, you're pitching strong,
    You ripped your pants, your putts are long.

You corrected for that uphill slice,
    You got a hook and skulled it twice.

You hit some fat shots, topped a few,
    They can't believe it's happening to you.

Advice is cheap or free I think,
    "Lay off awhile and have a drink."

If that won't work then we all know,
    There is always help from our local Pro.

LIMERICK

There was a small guy from the East,
Who lashed at that ball like a beast.
You'd have to admit,
At times he could hit,
But his score was a famine or feast.

WALKING TALL

There really is more to the game of golf,
Than the striking of the ball.

It keeps us young and in good health,
In a sense, we're walking tall.

It teaches us timing and dexterity skills,
So we can be "swingers" 'til over the hill.

But the things about golf that are appealing to me
Are the straightforward fun and camaraderie.

OFF DAY

Golfing is an exacting game,
      For those strikers of the ball.
Just when your game is settling in,
      You're asking for a fall.

You may be a super putter,
      And a sure-shot with your wedge.
But once in awhile you lose your touch,
      And your putts hang on the edge.

Not just one putt or one pitch shot,
      I'm talking about a bunch.
You're feeling great and striking well,
      But your brain went out to lunch.

We should play bridge or take up chess,
      But we love this crazy game.
And I'll be the first one to confess,
      Without it, life's not the same.

I'm hooked, I'm drugged, I'm truly baptized,
      And I don't know how to quit.
So I'll just apologize to my partner,
      'Cause I didn't play worth a s . . .

GOOD GOLF

Summertime, and the livin's easy,
　　And our golf game should improve.
We practice hard, sometimes in the yard,
　　But it's still not in the groove.

I'd take up chess and checkers,
　　But my grandsons beat me there.
Dancing is too vigorous,
　　And my rhythm doesn't care.

Reading is still boring,
　　And with that there is no press.
I'll just stay with a shorter game,
　　And practice for finesse.

It's just a game, like hell it is,
　　It's a "humble pie" escape.
So if I want to experience good golf,
　　I'll go home and watch a tape.

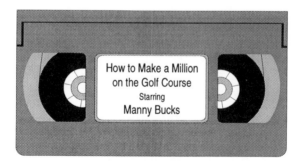

How to Make a Million
on the Golf Course
Starring
Manny Bucks

THAT PERFECT SHOT

How sweet it is to drive it straight,
    With just a little draw.
Especially on the number two tee,
    As others watch in awe.

And then your second shot to come,
    Is setting up real good.
As you walk up, it's plain to see,
    You do not need a wood.

Just a solid seven iron,
    To the fat part of the green.
It is that special kind of shot,
    You all know what I mean.

You line up with an open stance,
    Your hands slightly ahead.
You check your grip and waggle some,
    And move your feet a thread.

You start your backswing, low and slow,
    Your body starts to move.
A hesitation at the top,
    And now it's in the groove.

Your body turns, your arms uncork,
    And your wrists begin to snap.
You hit down hard into the ball,
    And it flies right o'er the trap.

It finds the green right near the pin,
    And the backspin pulls it back.
But you don't see the ball go in,
    'Cause you wake up in the sack.

GOLF ETIQUETTE

Our foursome meets three times a week,
    To grind out 18 holes.
As golfers go, we look the part,
    Nice clubs and sporty clothes.

We help each other with our games,
    But still we're out for blood.
We compliment each shot that's made,
    Even when it's just a dud.

We're quiet when each guy tees off,
    And courteously we watch 'em.
But when that poor guy starts to putt,
    He's waiting on a "gotchem."

PROVISIONAL BALL

I hit a ball into the rough,
    It could be in some trouble.
So now I'll hit a provisional ball,
    And get back on the bubble.

My second shot drops near the pin,
    I'll be one over par.
So please don't find the first one hit,
    It must have gone too far.

But alas they find that little jewel,
    In trouble plain to see.
Could end up with a five or six,
    On a hole that's just par three.

Had I not "announced" I'd hit a second,
    I couldn't play the first.
And in this series of scrambling,
    My first was much the worst.

So read the book and concentrate,
    On the ever faithful rule.
Now in this case, I'm better off,
    But most times I'm the fool.

OUR CLUB

A changing game since we play 'em down,
    The way it was designed.
In time will help improve our scores,
    Which helps me be inclined

To brag a bit about our club,
    And the beauty of our course.
Then drink a toast to maintenance,
    And our Board who are the source

For most improvements and more grass.
    Our fairways are looking great,
And sprinkler head yardages help a lot,
    These things we appreciate.

The steps are great, the fountains neat,
    They add a touch of class.
The greens will hold but roll quite well,
    You could say that some are fast.

What a feeling when you hit,
    To walk up to your ball.
And see that sphere of white or orange,
    Sitting up clean and tall.

A quote of pride, "we're on the move,"
    As we thank our volunteers.
Let's not forget our office staff,
    Who deserve a round of cheers.

Our pro shop folks are super nice,
    They help to lead the way.
They make this addictive game of golf,
    A game we love to play.

If I had a choice to make,
    And had to choose between
Giving up my lunch each day,
    Or giving up the green,

I'd surely choose the game of golf,
    And never hesitate.
Not only would I still have fun,
    I might even lose some weight.

QUESTIONS

Non-golfers seem to be confused,
    About the likes of us.
Just how a short missed birdie putt,
    Could cause someone to fuss.

And why it's called a birdie,
    When there aren't any wings.
And why a birdie is better than par,
    When par means better things.

The many questions that they ask,
    Are amusing and really neat.
Like why the spikes are necessary?
    Aren't they heavy on our feet?

Why all that extra exercise?
    And why that heavy bag?
Why not three clubs and a couple of balls,
    So there isn't so much drag?

Why the dimples on the balls?
    And what is this thing called "waggle?"
The club house deck has more allure,
    With coffee and a bagel.

Now what's a hook and what's a slice?
    They seem to cramp our style.
And then we end up at the start,
    With a ball we've chased a mile.

I guess the biggest question,
    Since we claim we never win,
Is why in the world we'd come back tomorrow,
    And do it all again?

METAL WOOD

I bought myself a "metal wood,"
    Now isn't that ridiculous?

If you believe there's a "metal wood,"
    You'll believe that I'm Jack Nicklaus.

BIG FOUR

The fundamentals of the game
      Are listed as "Big Four."
The grip, the stance, the take-away
      And the downswing helps you score.

There is of course a proper way
      That you should make this move.
But the variations you will find
      Are a jab, a slash, no groove.

Now I have seen some waggles
      That looked like grinds or bumps.
With backswings over emphasized,
      Flying elbows, twisting rumps.

Try to relax with a comfortable stance
      And slowly accelerate.
As the club passes through they say it is true,
      You should swing like an ol' garden gate.

Try swinging the club with just one hand,
      It's amazing what you see.
'Twill surprise you just how far it goes
      And it gives you a swing that's free.

Align your stance and grip the club
      With a firmish gentle grip.
Then make your turn, not with your arms,
      But by turning from the hip.

With a lot of patient practice
       You'll be swinging in the groove.
And cure some things like looking up,
       Or a head that wants to move.

Don't you dare to give it up,
       It's fun when hitting right.
Like walking into a darkened room
       And turning on a light.

Your peace of mind for a lower score
       Is something you will treasure.
And next to losing weight, my friend,
       It's a downright promised pleasure.

PLAY ON
THROUGH

PLAY ON THROUGH

The other day we were playing a match
    And hitting it really well.
When we caught up with a foursome,
    Beginners you could tell.

They said that we could play on through,
    Since they were playing slow.
And waited on the tee for us,
    So we could hit and go.

Concentration is a must,
    To really hit it all.
As I lined up, a remark I heard,
    "He hits a real long ball."

Human nature stepped right up,
    "These folks you must impress."
So I checked my grip and then my stance
    To have the right address.

I dragged it back and made my turn,
    Intent on smashing through.
And started down with all my force,
    They'd see what I could do.

All went well 'til I looked up,
    Which caused one fateful hitch.
My shoulder dropped, I hit it fat,
    And dribbled that son-of-a bitch.

PIN PLACEMENT

The placement of our pins are marked,
In colors just for you.
Red up front, white the center,
And the farthest back is blue.

Now if at last you're having fun,
And your attitude is par.
You still could win if you roll the dice,
At our friendly bar.

GO OUT IN STYLE

I don't want to live forever,
But just a little while.
Like 90 years among my peers,
And then go out in style.

I'd like to go on the 15th tee,
Facing the evening sun.
Just after hitting my finest shot,
That ends as a hole-in-one.

STROKE SAVER

On your drive just strike the ball,
"Don't let out on the shaft."
'Twill save you "blokes" a raft of strokes,
And a painful hemorrhoid graft.

ACE-I-FIED

A Hole In One, a special shot,
    A coveted stroke for those who've not.

To the ace-i-fied player we drink a toast,
    This is your day to brag or boast.

If not reported, our system's defeated,
    And most of all we all get cheated.

No celebration, no drinks for us,
    Not many congrats to the lucky cuss.

So report those aces to our friendly bar,
    So we can drink to the ace-holed star.

Our management team will follow up,
    In voicing congrats as we raise a cup.

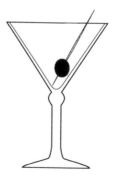

HOW SWEET IT IS

I've bought new clubs, I've bought new shoes,
And I've bought new balls
that I can use.

I've got desire and the old "Golf Pizazz,"
And I've changed that word from
"had" to "has."

I'm hittin' it straight and pickin' it clean,
And in regulation I'm on the green.

Now that's just great and fortune gives,
To those who putt -- "How sweet it is."

But if you're short or run it past,
The rest of your game will seem "half-fast."

FORE!

His grip is right, his stance is good,
His backswing low and slow.
He starts his turn, his left hand leads,
That ball should really go.

Now on this well-developed swing,
One thing I failed to tell.
As he uncoiled, someone yelled "fore,"
And he blew that shot to hell!

USE WHAT YOU'VE GOT

I've heard them argue the brand of ball,
 They drive and putt and pitch.
But I'll bet before they've gone 18 holes,
 It's a little white son-of-a-bitch.

And I've heard them brag about their clubs,
 With that little white ball they pound.
I've seen that group throw 'em up in "the soup,"
 And grab 'em and beat on the ground.

So use what you've got and practice a lot,
 If you want to score easy and smooth.
On your game you can dwell or say "What the hell,
 It's fun, just forget there's a groove."

BIG BERTHA

There is a new club called Big Bertha,
That propels that small ball off the eartha.
It soars like an eagle,
And should be illegal,
But it proves distance comes from inertia.

SET-UP
TERMINOLOGY

Outside, inside, target line,
      Open, squared, closed and align.
Shallow, steep, accelerate,
      Tempo, timing, compensate.
Unwinding, ball flight, level turn,
      Knee flex, posture, and you learn
To strike the ball and make it spin,
      Stick out your butt instead of in.
Parallel lines and left side clear.
      The club head path will help you hear
That special click hit on the screws.
      You're catching on, which lights the fuse
To more explosions off the tee,
      And makes boring practice worthwhile,
      you see.

LADIES' CLUBS

The buying of new golf clubs,
    Is really quite a chore.
Because to fit you properly,
    A golf pro you implore.

You get your swing weight all worked out,
    And how stiff you need the shaft.
And then decide which brand you like,
    With head weight fore or aft.

You also need to know which grip,
    And the shaft length for your height.
If you have a normal swing,
    And if you're left or right.

So after all this figuring,
    You pick out "Ping" or "Ram."
The first round that you play with them,
    You don't do worth a damn.

You could go on vacation,
    To work out with your sticks.
But you'd hit some good shots now and then,
    And you'd still have things to fix.

So don't despair, you'll get it there,
    It's just a game of skill.
Things could be worse, like losing your purse,
    Or forgetting to take the pill.

PLAYOFF

The eighteenth hole, we'd hit our first,
    And were laying side by side.
It was all tied up and I was "pumped,"
    I'd give that ball a ride.

I turned on concentration,
    And made a well-grooved swing.
I sure did smack that little ball,
    A really beautiful thing.

It soared in the air like an eagle,
    And checked up very quick,
And backed up just a little,
    And hit that ol' flag stick.

Bet you think I won it,
    But sorry, no such luck.
I'd hit the other fellow's ball,
    What a pain down in my gut.

So always check your golf ball,
    For your personal satisfaction.
'Cause "two strokes" hurt or "loss of hole,"
    Will put you out of action.

The rules are made for everyone,
    And at times may seem unfair.
But when they work to help you out,
    You're glad that they are there.

KEEPING IT CLASSY

In playing golf we've got it all,
      Beauty, friendship, hit the ball.

The twilight zone, we relate to that,
      As we strike some thin and strike
          some fat.

We always have the desire to win,
      Doing 18 holes with Vicodin.

But in senior golf we'd like to see,
      A lot more chatter on the tee,

Just to retain our poise and class,
      'Cause it's so embarrassing when
          we pass gas.

TURN THE
BIG DOG LOOSE

You drive for show and putt for dough,
    You've always heard them say.
And when you stand and watch awhile,
    You'll find it goes that way.

I know a guy who bought new woods,
    With the swing-weight changed a hair.
He practiced hard, but to no avail,
    The sweet spot wasn't there.

He tried more body turn at first,
    And then he changed his grip.
He moved the ball and checked his stance,
    And the direction of his hip.

At last he quit his painful search,
    And let out on the shaft.
If this goes on and he should miss,
    He'll need a "bunghole graft."

CALL OF THE TEE

Golf is an intriguing special game,
    It holds you like a vice.
It seems to enlarge your choice of words,
    And most of them ain't nice.

You play upon a well-mown course,
    Which is always an equalizer.
It warps your mind 'til you become
    More skillful and much wiser.

It lures you out into the rain,
    And under scorching sun.
It saps your strength and vital signs,
    And yet we call it fun.

So roll your butt out of the sack,
    Your foursome is on the tee.
The bets are made and strokes are sought,
    They've even paid your fee.

Just loosen up with one quick swing,
    And never mind the chatter.
It's eighteen holes of fun and fraud,
    And your handicap doesn't matter.

You play your best and concentrate,
    And show them you can score.
And give to them what they planned for you,
    Just cut them to the core.

Strike that driver on the screws,
Right straight on down the stretch.
Your second wood is just up short,
You should be hard to catch.

You pitch the ball and make it run,
But you forget it's number two.
And as you watch in sinking horror,
Your ball rolls back to you.

This uphill putt for a needed par,
Will take a jeweler's touch.
Be positive and stroke it firm,
Don't hold it like a crutch.

Square to square and firmly stroked,
Smoothly past your hip.
Your mouth goes dry, you had it made,
But it stopped right on the lip.

What can you say, it's just not your day,
But never once show that you care.
If it should continue, practice a bit,
You always can call "Dial-A-Prayer."

CHAPTER 3

RUB
OF THE GREEN

CLUBS

If you analyze your golf clubs,
      You'll find they give release.
They also give you lots of pain,
      But when you win, there's peace.

Your driver builds your ego up,
      When you hit it down the pike.
But when you hook it off the tee,
      It creates a great dislike.

Your 3-wood is your fairway tool,
      It's magic when hit right.
But when you hit it fat or thin,
      You're mad enough to fight.

Long irons are a testing group,
      They take a lot of poise.
But should you hurry with your swing,
      Your words will shock the boys.

Now mid-irons are utilities,
      They bridge the fairway gap.
But when you pick 'um thin and hard,
      They fly clear off the map.

Short irons are the stock-in-trade,
      They set up for the putt.
It takes finesse and feel, my friend,
      Or you won't make the cut.

Now if in sand you find yourself,
    It will take a special tool.
And if you leave it in the trap,
    You'll call yourself a fool.

And then your putter, what a club,
    It answers all your prayers.
But if it's off you're all shook up,
    And recovery is rare.

You use these clubs like the game of life,
    With occasionally a trap.
You play the game just for yourself,
    'Cause who else gives a crap?

MY GAME

I get so damned disgusted,
      Can't get my game together.
My game reminds me very much,
      Of San Francisco weather.

Some days I really hit it well,
      No trouble off the tee.
And then my irons I'm screwing up,
      A problem plain to see.

I practice hard on all my irons,
      Until I am content.
I play a round to try them out,
      'Cause now I'm pleasure bent.

Now you guessed it, I give up,
      I just don't have the goods.
I'm hitting irons just like a dream,
      And I'm screwing up my woods.

I think I'll take up alcohol,
      And change my life a bit.
And find a place where I can booze,
      Where golf is not "a hit."

But with my luck, even that won't work,
      I'd pick the wrong damned bar.
And some inebriated guy would say,
      "You don't look up to par."

THE DIVOT

A divot is a piece of grass,
    With soil attached, you see.
Now some of us take hefty ones,
    On the course it's plain to see.

There are more of us and that's more strokes,
    So please lend me your ears.
Our course is showing battle scars,
    That every golfer fears.

I know - it's happening to me at times,
    And I'll bet you find them, too.
And those who hit from a divot hole,
    And hit it good are few.

Please take your sand and seed along,
    And fix 'em as you play.
'Twill grow right back, please join the pack,
    So our lies are good each day.

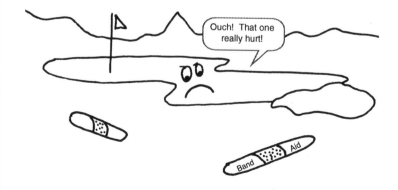

Balls 4 Sale
Real
Cheep

GOPHER

In lots of places on the course,
     Where swingin' golfers play.
There lives a little animal,
     That we all see every day.

He's just a furry fellow,
     Who lives down in a hole.
And as I wait to hit the ball,
     I wonder what's his goal.

I prefer this kind of animal,
     To one that sneaks and crawls.
But as he lurks I have this feeling,
     He wants to grab my balls.

MALE GOLFER

The golfer is a special guy,
    With face of tan and bloodshot eye.

He plays each time to win a prize,
    But he usually gets just exercise.

He'll smash his drive with casual ease,
    While a 12-inch putt will make him freeze.

So when he comes home tired and mad,
    Please understand - he's just been had.

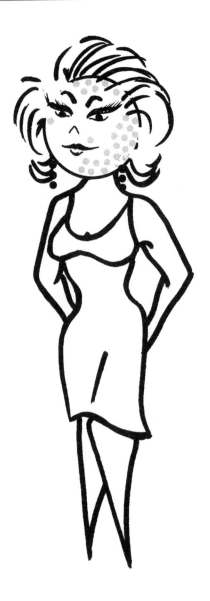

Oh, you beautiful doll.
You small round dimplified doll!

THE BALL

You attractive, curvaceous little doll,
    You woo us one and all.
How can you be so desirable,
    When you're just a stupid ball?

You cause us many hours of pain,
    For you we get cold and wet.
We swear at you and throw you out,
    But your charm we can't forget.

You drive us to distraction,
    And help us lose our butt.
And then you woo us back again,
    With a side-hill birdie putt.

It blows our minds the "clout" you have,
    Since you're turned out from a press.
You have the following of a movie star,
    With no goal and no finesse.

You may have dimples on your "bod,"
    And you always go first class.
So what's your secret "little doll,"
    To make us lose our ass?

DREAMER

If fate would grant you just one wish,
I know what you would do.
You'd take your clubs and fly away,
To a golfing rendezvous.

You'd sleep and bask 'til nine o'clock,
When the dew is off the grass,
And then you'd eat and rent a cart,
And play golf on your pass.

But then each night you'd drink a few,
And watch the tropic moon,
Then steal away to meditate,
In some gal's cozy room.

But don't you dare! That golfin' gal
Can be the sucker's bait.
To prove my point so you won't go,
A story I will relate.

He met a gal the first day there,
Who liked his style and swing.
And since she liked the game of golf,
He helped her "do her thing."

He checked her stance and waggle, too,
As she kept pouring booze.
When he awoke, he was dead broke,
With nothing but his shoes.

"Sorry 'bout the 'mickey,' " she wrote,
   "Before we got to play.
The devil made me do it, Hon,
   That's how I earn my pay."

So when you're golfin' away from home,
   Don't help those in distress.
Believe me, Dad, you'll just "get had,"
   Before you start your press.

PUTTING

The putting stroke without a doubt
  Controls each golfer's score.
More than any part of the golfing game
  Since they started yelling "fore."

It seems no one has yet agreed
  On the grip or stance or roll.
Or should you punch or stroke the ball,
  Or just "rap it in the hole."

Most folk know to keep it low,
  And hit it square and clean.
But when there's pressure, you will find,
  That "pesky" three-putt green.

As in this match the golfer had
  The winning three-foot putt.
Which caused a muscle spasm;
  You're right, he lost his butt!

SWINGER

A golfer is the nicest guy,
　　　You'd ever want to meet.
With suntanned face and friendly smile,
　　　And manners so discreet.

His casual walk and easy style,
　　　Hide power that's emergin'.
He enjoys the feeling "he can win,"
　　　'Cause to losing he's no virgin.

He'd rather golf than eat, they say,
　　　Filets, champagne or custard.
And he'll be swinging those ol' sticks,
　　　When he's too old to cut the mustard.

THE SWING

Slowing your backswing, then down and through,
  Will produce a shot that is long and true.

But if you rush any part of your swing,
  The ball will falter and not do its thing.

Relax and just swing like a well-oiled gate,
  Improving your shots to help compensate

For all those shots that have gone astray,
  'Twill make you feel glad that you
      came out today.

Arnie has his armies,
          He's a golfing pioneer.
He set the stage for modern golf,
          Which increases every year.

He won his share while on the tour,
          Now the senior tour and skins.
He has that same old "go for it,"
          And we're proud each time he wins.

Thank you Arnie for your push,
          We're glad you've stayed around.
To encourage us to keep playing golf,
          'Til we're six feet underground.

THE BOOK

I got myself a different book,
     Shows how to hypnotize.
Will help you play much better golf,
     In a way you'll be surprised.

It tells you how you should relax,
     Through your subconscious mind.
Your swing improves, you strike it good,
     And you hit it down the line.

You do this when you go to bed,
     You lay real quiet and straight.
You tell your wife, "Please not tonight,
     I have to meditate."

You start relaxing every part,
     Starting with your toes.
Next with your feet, your legs, your thighs,
     Gets better as it goes.

When you've relaxed 'most every part,
     Except your head and ears.
You tell yourself to count to ten,
     And curb your sleeping gears.

Sleep will try to creep in fast,
     Before your count is done.
Instruct yourself to concentrate,
     On your golf game when it's fun.

A mental picture of your game,
    When you are swinging right.
And tell yourself "I will improve."
    Now do this every night.

They claim it works if you will try,
    To do it for a week.
I'd guess by then your wife is mad,
    And probably won't speak.

To offset this, you're feeling great,
    You're beating all the guys.
It feels real good to see them dig,
    Amidst their groans and cries.

I haven't won a big amount,
    And it hasn't cured my hook.
But I've won enough to ease my pain,
    And pay for this damned book.

I'll rent this book for 50 cents,
    Or two weeks for a buck.
And you can tell how well it works,
    When they say "your score is luck."

Each night I'm sleeping in a trance,
    And thinking about my game.
My wife doesn't seem to understand,
    That she has this book to blame.

It may not work for everyone,
    No need to take a poll.
But I'm not knockin' "anything,"
    That helps get it in the hole.

WONDER PLANT

Living in Utopia,
      Is not a perfect spot,
Because we have some "put-downs,"
      Whether we like it or not.

The pesky one that's always there,
      To threaten and aggravate,
Is poison oak, the wonder plant,
      How can we eradicate?

We spray it and we dig it up,
      With Round-Up and the pick.
We walk around it, wash our clothes,
      And think we have it licked.

But as we sit to read the news,
      Or watch our favorite show,
An itch will start that wasn't there,
      A few short hours ago.

So if you do not hit it straight,
      And your ball goes left or right,
Watch out when you go to pick it up,
      Or it's poison oak tonight.

Don't give up - keep fighting it,
      And dig up each new batch.
Then get a shot if it persists,
      Or keep some just to scratch.

GAMBLER

Somebody said it couldn't be done,
But he was a wagerin' guy.
So he pulled out a wood and smoked it again,
And hit that green on the fly.

Now don't be envious of the shot he made,
To hit a par five in just two.
You know from the past that your luck doesn't last,
You guessed it - that shot wasn't through.

His shot had the flight, but a wood just won't bite,
And it bounced to a bunker below.
He still kept his cool, a real bettin' fool,
As he struck his sand wedge crisp to go.

It came out red hot and rolled by a lot,
And ended way out on the berm.
So now as he chips, it rolls by the lip,
And he's four and beginning to burn.

To bet on a shot with what talent we've got,
Is like "making out" three times a day.
It's great at the time, but to finish this rhyme,
If you can't cut the mustard, you pay.

THE OVER-FIFTY ODE

Some think you'd give the damned game up,
     As you struggle to win or lose.
But you'd be lost without the sport,
     And it keeps you less confused.

'Cause it's "never up - never in,"
     And "stroke it in the hole."
And if your sights are "victory,"
     You'd better change your goal.

To bogey golf and temper booze,
  If you are over fifty.
They say that those are the "golden years,"
  And you're not old but "nifty."

Those "golden years" - ain't that a blast,
  It makes your temper boil.
Directions are printed in the smallest type,
  And everything's sealed in foil.

You start to have more aches and pains
  And your bowels begin to wheeze.
So I'd suggest some Old Grandad,
  Chased with lots of cheese.

Do you usually hurt when you get up?
  Do your joints all seem to ache?
Are your fingers stiff when you try to putt
  That may cause you to miss "that snake?"

Do you have a problem with reading small print?
  Are your reflexes a'way too slow?
Do they think that you are holding back,
  When actually you "let 'er go?"

Do you really enjoy this getting old
  With everything "in a jiff?"
Do you realize all the reverses you have,
  When the wrong damned things get stiff?

"Grow old," they say, "gracefully,"
  As the retirement years sneak past.
Take that "gracefully through the 'golden years' "
  And stick it up their ass.

YOU'RE A PRO

Did you ever dream that you're a Pro?
    No, not a prophylaxis.
A Pro that plays golf on the tour,
    With a caddie who helps you practice.

I know you're not out there on the tour,
    Nor do you have a caddie.
But you are a Pro 'cause you play 'em all,
    And some are mighty "ratty."

Touring pros have everything,
    Like fairways tailor-made.
They travel 'round the countryside,
    And play their draw or fade.

But they don't have the comradeship,
    Like guys who play with us.
Our guys have manners and finesse,
    And never drink or cuss.

You never see us throw a club,
    Or bitch if we should miss.
Or drive our carts too damned fast,
    Or use a tree to p. . . .

We fix ball marks and rake the traps,
    And go by all the rules.
You'll find that we all play real hard,
    We are far from being fools.

We play 'em down out in the rough,
    In blue or bermuda grass.
And usually go up one club,
    And swing from out our ass.

It makes us hit 'em straight-away,
    With determined concentration.
And eliminate the need to have,
    A hernia operation.

You normally swing "a grooved-type shot,"
    With stepped up acceleration.
But in the rough it's "from the top,"
    From pent up aggravation.

FIRST POEM

It's funny how your practice swing,
Is better than your hit.
I knocked that pine cone half a mile,
But my drive's not worth a s...!

NO PERMANENT SATISFACTION

We play this crazy game of golf,
For its challenge and its action.
But just like sex and lemonade,
There's no permanent satisfaction.

RELIEF

Should my poems start to bore you,
Or if you have to pee.
Just jump right up and ambulate
And relieve that misery.

APPROACH

IT'S JUST A GAME - 1

Now someone said the other day,
　　"So what, it's just a game."
The dirty, rotten, stinkin' sport,
　　It really is insane.

But we all keep on coming back,
　　To play it in the grass.
And may not quit until we grow,
　　A flag-stick out our ass.

LIMERICK

There was a nice guy from L.A.
Who truly enjoyed golf to play.
　　Now no one would guess,
　　That he would transgress,
And cheat on his score every day.

HOLE-N-ONE

A hole in one is having fun,
 The best things in life are free.
After playing tough hole number two,
 You can ace our number three.

We've had a few from the beautiful view,
 On easy hole number seven,
And were you slated for fiery hell,
 That ace gets you to heaven.

Now playing on, we're all upon
 The struggling golfer's shelf.
And striking a ball with flawless skill,
 You can ace old number twelve.

More drinks, me thinks, with each new ace,
 And two more holes between.
The view, the lake, you demonstrate,
 You ace-i-fied fifteen.

Some aces happen away from home.
 These also go on a plaque
That honor our distinguished "aces group,"
 Which keeps us coming back

To have a chance to get free drinks,
 And enjoy this special place.
And hope the gods will smile on us,
 So we can score an ace.

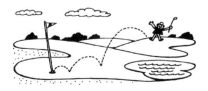

IT'S JUST A GAME - II

It's just a game! - **like hell it is,**
     In a game, you have some fun.
You laugh and smile and enjoy yourself,
     And you're happy when it's done.

But when you hook shots out-of-bounds
     Or slice them to the right,
I write this poem for losers all,
     Gathered here tonight.

To hell with fat shots falling short,
     And sculled shots down the pike.
Damn the chip shots across the green,
     And shoes that lose a spike.

And when you get it on the green,
     That little white pesky ball,
Think positive and stroke it firm,
     And they say that it will fall.

But if you plan to improve your putts
     And think your slump will pass,
Unless you practice, you'll putt as well
     With your driver from the grass.

IT'S HARD TO BE HUMBLE

Oh, Lord, but it's hard to be humble,
     When you just parred the Spy Glass front nine.
And you didn't get wet, hardly worked up a sweat,
     And you're taking your wife out to dine.

Oh, Lord, but it's hard to be humble,
     When most things are going so right.
When your medicine works and hardly anything hurts,
     And you didn't get up in the night.

Oh, Lord, but it's hard to be humble,
     When you dress like a golfer on tour.
The choose-ups you've played and the
         winners you've paid,
     And for your slice or your push there's a cure.

Oh, Lord, but it's hard to be humble,
     With this weather and golf course so great.
You can play all day long and you feel you belong,
     And your wife understands when you're late.

GOLF VERSUS FISHING

A day without golf is a wasted day,
    And that's my kind of wishing.
Our professional, Willie, will not agree,
    'Cause for him, he'd rather be fishing.

In golf there's no loading and unloading the boat,
    And that fish smell that constantly lingers.
Then when it's time to eat your sack lunch,
    You can't even lick off your fingers.

In golfing we have the nicest green grass,
    And no waiting for something to bite.
You just play your game in pleasant attire,
    With satisfaction when you're hitting it right.

So give me a golf club instead of a rod,
    And I'll end each nice day with a putt.
No scaling and cleaning the catch of the day,
    With my drink I'll settle down on my butt.

TO THE TUNE OF "BILL BAILEY"

Won't you come home, Bill Bailey?
Won't you come home?
You've played the whole day long.
I know you're hooking badly and hitting fat,
And all your putts are strong.
I remember that fateful evening,
That you got the shanks.
And now your whole game's wrong.
I know it's a shame,
And your Pro is to blame.
Bill Bailey, won't you please come home?
("I'm in my nightie.")
Bill Bailey, won't you please come home?

LIVE IT UP,
THE PAIN WILL PASS

I'm so glad we came today,
    It's really been a blast.
The weather's tops, our group is great,
    And the greens were all half fast.

Was another chance to live a bit,
    And hit that stupid ball.
It beats the hell out of sittin' round,
    And loafin' at the mall.

As we get old, the scene will change,
    And we'll wonder what's up next.
'Cause when you're young you smack the ball,
    And there's unrestricted sex.

So tee it up - play all you can,
    And remember your past dreams.
'Cause even though there's mental zeal,
    It ain't just like it seems.

The ball doesn't seem to roll as far,
        The stairs, they seem so long.
And making love is too relaxed,
        Like the chorus of a song.

The melody is just the same,
        And the lyrics still are nice,
But it seems the down beat has less "oomph,"
        And you seldom play it twice.

Practice helps you strike the ball,
        And improves your waning game.
But practice or not, play right now,
        And your life will stay the same.

'Cause exercise and sun are great,
        With age it's like vermouth.
It has a soothing aftermath,
        Like the freshness from your youth.

We hope you had a real good round,
        And didn't lose your ass.
But losing is like kidney stones,
        The pain will always pass.

A BUMMER

I wonder why we play this game,
    At times it is a "bummer."
It has a coaxing tempting trait,
    Through winter and hot summer.

We freeze our hands, get soaking wet,
    But still keep that desire.
In heat of summer men all sweat,
    But the ladies just perspire.

Our aches and pains don't seem as bad,
    When out there we feel "swell."
But cleaning house or chopping wood,
    Our joints all hurt like hell.

The pain pills help a little bit,
    'Bout four hours at the most.
Who'd ever dreamed when we were young,
    We'd need aspirin with our toast?

And again at noon and bedtime too,
    Quote "Did you take your pills?"
Our biggest project since retiring,
    Is prescriptions and refills.

So diligently we all come back,
    And concentrate on par.
And a great solution when we lose,
    Is a cold one at the bar.

HOW WAS YOUR DAY?

The dirty rotten stinking game,
    We love it with a passion.
It brings out all the worst in us,
    As we wear the latest fashion.

We find out if we have control,
    Of our temper and our tongue.
It's a challenging human equalizer,
    That keeps us thinking young.

The courses that we're apt to play,
    Are a changing picture scene.
It's a mini-vacation each time we play,
    So peaceful and serene.

We folk who play are super nice,
    Or we clown around like nuts.
We never cuss or criticize,
    And always give three-inch putts.

We never talk when it's time to hit,
    We never walk behind.
We always say "A nice shot, Friend,"
    Which proves that we are blind.

We pay our bets most graciously,
    And never bitch a bit.
But when our spouses ask how it went,
    We say "Not worth a s . . ."

PARTED YOUTH

Oh, how we yearn for parted youth,
        To have that reflex back.
We'd hit that ball a country mile,
        And learn how to relax.

So play this game for all it's worth,
        And chuckle at your score.
It gets no better than we have it here,
        Who could ask for anything more?

MODERN GOLF

The game of golf has much for us,
        For some it turns us on.
While others play to get away,
        Instead of mowing the lawn.

In the language of the younger set,
        With golf "I found my thing."
It's "really great," it's "fabulous,"
        And it always feels like spring.

Outsiders watch with doubtful eyes,
        They think we've gone the route.
Because in golf, the super sport,
        We "let 'er all hang out."

CAN'T HAVE IT ALL

When I'm out there on the course,
    God knows that I'm a nut.
And I'm real sure that He is there,
    Until I miss a putt.

And then I say, "What happened, Lord?
    I need You every shot."
And with my faith I can't believe
    My game has gone to pot.

And then within, a soft kind voice
    Says, "Do you need it all?
You have good health and nature's best,
    And you're free, **so hit the ball**."

HOOKED

In golf there're several winners,
      But most guys lose their butts.
And the mutual thing most golfers have,
      Are tired bods 'n empty guts.

And ladies, we are sorry,
      If we oft times make you wait.
But as long as your old man is hooked,
      I'm afraid this is your fate.

Please put up with this problem,
      Until it cramps your style.
Then plan "your game" much the same,
      And cut him off awhile.

I should know, 'cause I'm the Joe,
      Who said, "Golf is such a hex."
I had in mind cut off my food,
      But don't cut off my sex.

Life would be so very dull,
If there were no golf at all!

Mary had a little lamb,
    And golfing has its groups.
Arnie has his army,
    And Trevino has his troops.

They both are reeking with ability,
    And definitely show more class.
They hit the ball much further than I,
    'Cause they both throw in more ass.

ENJOY NOW

About the time we have the time,
    To relax and really play.
Something quits within our "bod,"
    And tries to spoil our day.

A knee, a hip, our eyes or ears,
    And sometimes even our heart.
And if we're missing anything,
    They will even add a part.

T'ain't funny, Folks, it slows us down,
    So we can't do our thing.
But we're not coming this way again,
    So let's give it everything.

GOLDEN YEARS

The aging years are trying times,
       Depending where we are.
Finances place us in a group,
       Unless we are a "star."

By "star" I mean a winner, Friend,
       Someone who made it big.
At 55 they "have it made,"
       No snow they have to dig.

The normal guy just plugs along,
       Pays taxes, takes his knocks.
And if he tries to hang it up,
       He could go on the rocks.

So give the aging lots of room,
       Don't put them on the shelf.
Because you'll find it sneaks up on you,
       And you get old yourself.

Your memory is the first to go,
       And then you start to sag.
The steps get long, your breath gets short,
       You need to wear a tag

That says "Behold, I'm getting old,"
       But still I'm shifting gears.
And then some jerk who's "over-perked,"
       Calls these "The Golden Years."

The "golden years," that silly nut,
       He should be boiled in oil.
When even the vitamins that we take,
       Are sealed up tight with foil.

I wonder if he shovels snow,
    Or even mows his yard.
I wonder if he's pushin' dope,
    Or somehow he's inspired.

We're over-aged, over-taxed,
    And overjoyed to be
Just playing golf and drinking beer,
    On our 19th Tee.

MacDonald's gives us "free-bee" drinks,
    Sometimes our tax is paid.
I never dreamed of a motel discount,
    With hot and cold running maids.

They give the aged lots of things,
    But a lot no one can use.
Like contraceptives and toothpaste,
    No teeth and sex defused.

They give out aids to help our hair,
    And aids to help our tummy.
If we're not bald, we're losing it,
    Our health-aides are really funny.

I wonder what they'll think of next,
    Knowing we're desperate and a sucker.
I'd prefer they help our aching feet,
    And a pill for rectal pucker.

I'd rather call it what it is,
    And aim us at the sky.
The shuttle is our only hope,
    Where there's always room to fly.

It worries me a trifle,
    That we are dealt this hand.
Because most guys in Washington,
    Are "old" and run our land.

FIRST THINGS FIRST

A golf vacation is just the thing
In some exclusive spot.

You're feelin' good, you're havin' fun
And your golf game's really hot.

You're in the playoff at this club,
You feel you can't be beat.

But the night before, oh fickle fate,
Your wife just came "in heat."

HERE'S TO THE GUY

Here's to the guy with ball so clean,
　　　Who wants to get it on the green.
He screws up several shots he hits,
　　　His reward's an O'Douls or Schlitz.

Here's to the guy who does it all,
　　　Who really pounds that little ball.
His handicap is even scratch,
　　　His reward - can't get a match!

Here's to the guy who plays for fun,
　　　Doesn't know his score when done.
He will never win a prize.
　　　His reward - just exercise!

DON'T QUIT

My back is sore, my wrist is stiff,
     It's been a long, long day.
On this I blame my lousy score,
     But still enjoyed the play.

I'll do it every chance I get,
     To play and do my thing.
It may not be a work of art,
     But still it is a swing.

It may not stay within the groove,
     But yet I'll try it all.
And concentrate on stance and grip,
     To smack that small white ball.

When the 18 holes are finished,
     And I'm a "wee" bit over par.
The companionship and cool, cool drink,
     Are waiting at the bar.

IT'S JUST A GAME-III

Outsiders do not understand
    Why golfers love to play.
"You drive for show and putt for dough,"
    I've heard some players say.

One expression that we have
    Which keeps us from a "win,"
Sounds kinda ornery to some folks,
    "Never up and never in."

There are other quotes that we may hear
    While sitting in the bar.
Like "country club bounce" and "super snake"
    And "just a ho-hum par."

I played with a guy the other day
    Who struck the ball real sweet.
And he told of a fairway marker
    That said, "All you can eat."

So if you're playing by summer rules,
    And your ball lies in a hole,
Just hood that iron an extra bit,
    And pretend that you're a mole.

As my wife has always said to me,
    "It's just a game, why fizz?"
And my response is always the same,
    "A game, **like hell it is!**"

CHAPTER 5

STYMIED

SLOW PLAY

We have this little problem
      Of golfers playing slow.
And with our increasing membership,
      We must get up and go.

I have this small suggestion,
      Which is just another view.
The slow ones have to stand and wait,
      While the fast ones play on through.

If this suggestion doesn't work,
      And slow groups become a bunch.
We'll have the kitchen prepare a physic,
      To put in their sack lunch.

ADAM AND EVE

Adam surely was a golfer
        And the reason that this is true,
He gave his rib to Eve and taught
        Her strokes that were brand new.

Since then it's just reversed itself
        And the lady plays golf too,
And keeps the home fire burning,
        So that free rib sure came through.

KNOW THE SCORE

You'll never hit 'em all just right,
    Or have a low, low score.
But you can enjoy the game a lot,
    And keep coming back for more.

Don't move your head, just strike the ball,
    And then with follow-through,
You'll be surprised how nice it flies,
    And feels much better, too.

Golf is really a lot like life,
    You need a tender grip.
Life's happenings are much the same,
    As a ball hung on the lip.

Disappointing, I should say,
    It nearly brings the tears.
But then you snake one in the cup,
    And it wipes away your fears

That there's a chance you're losing it,
    And your game has gone to pot.
But it's still **the greatest game on earth**,
    Whether you win or not.

Continue to be a swinger, Friends,
    And age won't change a thing.
You might not keep your fluid drive,
    But the enjoyment is the same.

It may take longer to climb a hill,
    And for some there may be more.
But if you'll continue to play around,
    You'll always know the score.

HARRY

There was a golfer named Harry,
Who died in a game, how dare he.
Even though it was wrong,
They dragged him along,
He was just too heavy to carry.

"Well, William, you know what they say.
If you can't lick 'em, join 'em!"

LONG SUFFERING FELLOW

I hit a ball into the air,
    It fell to earth I know not where.

We looked and looked to no avail,
    It didn't even leave a trail.

It teed me off, I lost a stroke,
    And lost my butt, so now I'm broke.

But I'll come back to play again,
    To beat the guy with the winning grin.

'Cause golf's like life, it's up and down,
    It lifts you up, then plays the clown.

As mother nature casts her spell,
    And makes you fight that heavenly hell.

If I could have one wish today,
    It's nerve to give my clubs away.

So come on out and be a duffer,
    And join the group of those who suffer.

IF

"If" is such a little word,
　　　But as I watch folks at their game
Talking 'bout the rough and playing tough
　　　And the "if" things that they blame.

There are rotten lies and railroad ties,
　　　Or "my ball rolled off the cliff."
This stinking game that we call golf
　　　Is really a game called "If."

"If they hadn't hit that tree,"
　　　And "If that putt had fallen,"
Their handicap would be much lower,
　　　And they'd be happy instead of sullen.

But then, alas, that round is posted,
　　　And tomorrow seems gloomy black.
And then hooray, they make a "Bird,"
　　　Which keeps them coming back!

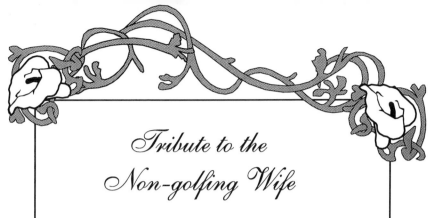

Tribute to the
Non-golfing Wife

The golfer's wife is the nicest gal
      You'll ever want to know.
She's a tolerant, sexy, wonder-gal
      Who really is "gung-ho."

Her idea of having fun
      Is wine and dine and dance.
Not playing golf in the boiling sun
      Or in soaking shoes and pants.

The weekends she will spend alone
      'Cause hubby's at the links.
And if he won he's riden' high,
      But if he lost he stinks.

She can't explain to everyone
      Why her man is golfin' prey.
But she understands most of the time
      What makes him want to play.

That's why at times he comes on strong,
      And this will end my sequel.
Because in golf or in sex,
      We're **not** created equal.

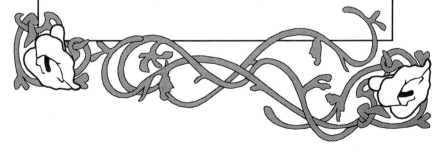

NIFTY GOLFERS

The Alta Sierra ladies,
     Have golfing in their blood.
And nothing stops their playing,
     Not downpour, snow or flood.

The weaker sex? Don't you believe it,
     Some walk these hills to play.
And still come in with a refreshing look,
     Like an ad out of "Woman's Day."

A little worn but most content,
     Unruffled in neat attire.
And unlike men, they do not sweat,
     They glow or perhaps perspire.

Hats off to you nice ladies,
     We're glad you do your thing.
And whether you ride or walk for health,
     You retain the blush of spring.

Don't give it up, it's good for you,
     And no doubt will make you stronger.
So with the glow it perpetuates,
     You're bound to live much longer.

HEAVENLY
GOLF

Oh, beautiful for spacious skies,
      Over greens that putt the same.
For fairways that are plush with grass,
      That really help your game.

For golf carts that will massage your legs,
      And cut your time in half.
And nylon golden colored flags,
      Upon a graphite staff.

Ball washers that will play a tune,
      To soothe you when you're mad.
And tees so green your small white ball,
      Will know that it's "been had."

And just for those who do partake,
      A mini-bar of sorts,
On every other hole, at least,
      So you can have those "snorts."

Now if you had this course to play,
      With sunshine six to seven.
You would no doubt have to assume,
      That this was golfer heaven.

You're right, my friend, it's not on earth,
      And maybe just as well.
'Cause you'd take your damned ol' hook or slice
      And blow your score to hell.

NEVER UP-NEVER IN

She met this dashing fellow,
    And they really hit it off.
Their interests seemed to be the same,
    Including the game of golf.

She did admit they lived it up,
    And played some practice rounds.
Before they decided on the date,
    For tux and wedding gowns.

And then at last the blissful night,
    They became new wedded folk.
But when he got upon the green,
    He lost his putting stroke.

We haven't solved his problem,
    But some tips we'll pass to you.
To play the game on or off the course,
    You've got to follow through.

And the normal position of the shaft,
    Is right above the ball.
It must be "firm" or some say "stiff,"
    Or you'll have no stroke at all.

So buy yourself a name brand ball,
    As it is advertised.
'Cause when you're counting on a long hard round,
    You want it energized.

And when you hit it off the tee,
    You're aiming for the pin.
As the saying goes by all the pros,
    "Never up and never in."

MEN ONLY

I had this premonition
      That my golf game could improve.
That every day if I practiced hard
      I'd swing it in the groove.

But the fickle finger of father fate
      Was standing with a squint.
And said "Old man, just give it up,
      'Cause you're not pleasure bent."

"You try too hard, you don't relax,
      And you're swingin' from the top."
He suggested a much slower turn,
      With follow-through, don't stop!

You may not end up quite as good
      As "swingin' Jerry Pate."
But you'll improve if you grip the club
      Just like you urinate.

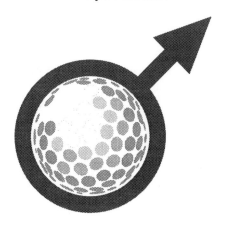

BASICS

Tee up your ball - don't look around,
And keep both feet upon the ground.

You cannot play the game of golf,
If from the ball your eye is off.

'Cause if you peek - no sweet spot hit,
Which means your shot's not worth a s...!

LIMERICK

There was a big guy from the Bay,
Who could knock that ol' ball far away.
One could surmise,
'Twas because of his size,
That his score was near par every day.

LETTING OUT
ON THE SHAFT

I think that I shall never see,
    A ball hit further off the tee.

It started low in a gradual lift,
    With a little hook it began to drift.

And when it hit, boy what a hop,
    With that overspin it couldn't stop.

A pained expression, not overjoyed,
    'Cause on the ground lay a hemorrhoid.

GOLF-ITIS

It seems I practice more and more,
      My game stands still and I get sore.

And even Santa at our door
      Won't leave golf gifts, but just yells "Fore."

Now do I quit from all of that,
      From a bright red suit on a guy that's fat?

That drives a sleigh and not a ball,
      And probably can't putt at all?

Hell no I don't and come the spring,
      I'll grab those clubs and do my thing.

DISTRACTIONS

Distractions in the game of golf,
      Cause many screwed up rounds.
Like trains, horns, low-flying planes,
      And even nature's sounds.

But I have noticed many times,
      A concentration must.
That when the fairer sex plays golf,
      In shorts with bouncin' bust.

You better make a mental block,
      Like in some vacuum tubes.
So if your ball flies at someone,
      You'll still yell "fore" not "boobs."

MONTEREY

Pebble Beach is a gorgeous place
    That sets the status of the golfing pace.

It's the golf course of our special dreams
    With all that beauty and a few extremes.

Now when you play the Spy Glass course
    You may go home with some remorse.

It's an enjoyable course that keeps you wishing,
    As Jack Nicklaus says, "I'd rather go fishing."

Then Spanish Bay, the perfect links,
    It's inspiring even when low tide stinks.

The bagpiper adds appealing class,
    An experience that enhances the crystal glass.

The Inn is spacious with its Scottish trend
    That makes you wish 'twill never end.

Thanks PGA for your far reaching vision,
    The trip to play was a rewarding decision.

You helped us all to compete and play,
    As the ex-mayor says, "You made our day."

You're the perfect host and we "had a ball,"
    Like soaring with eagles, we all walked tall.

'TIL THEY PUT YOU ON THE SHELF

Now some of us should spend more time,
    And practice on our game.
'Cause if we don't, our game will slip,
    And never be the same.

Hitting shags is boring work,
    But it always seems to pay.
Until you miss it on the course,
    Which makes a longer day.

So play as often as you can,
    And be good to yourself.
Take your pills and kiss your wife,
    'Til they put you on the shelf.

Practice Makes Perfect!

POSTING

A golf score card is a masterpiece,
    With entries of every kind.
There are dots and circles with squares and adjusts,
    It sure takes a mastermind.

Five hours to play, and then the real fun,
    Of deciphering and posting this "jewel."
You roll for the drinks and sometimes for food,
    If you win all this, you're no fool.

When you are posting, there's always a line,
    Poor eyesight makes glasses a must.
And the chatter you hear is a treat to your ear,
    For the most part the scores are a bust.

If I win a million from old Ed McMahon,
    And the chances of this are quite slim.
I'll buy a computer just for the Pro Shop,
    And we'll "post" as we turn our card in.

The code will be simple, a membership code,
    And you'll be in and out very fast.
The computer will store it for months at a time,
    With a total of "losing your ass."

FINALE

I hope that you enjoyed this book,
     And found your game in rhyme.
'Cause golf's a game of varied talents,
     Shown better in our prime.

Some are quick and some are slow,
     In this physical participation.
And some have tempers rather short,
     When not in syncopation.

A game, we know, of joy and stress,
     Depending on our goal.
For some a great relaxing sport,
     While others prefer to bowl.

The courses with their shades of green,
     Are scenes beyond compare.
The exercise and cooling breeze,
     Make us pleasantly aware

We could get hooked on this crazy game,
     And we won't know when to stop.
But if we love it as much as some,
     We will play until we drop.